ESSENTIAL

BRAZILIAN JIU JITSU

ESSENTIAL

BRAZILIAN JIU JITSU

Marc Walder

Library of Congress Cataloging-in-Publication Data

Walder, Marc.
  Essential Brazilian jiu jitsu / Marc Walder.
       p. cm.
  Includes index.
  ISBN-13: 978-0-7360-7488-9 (soft cover)
  ISBN-10: 0-7360-7488-0 (soft cover)
1. Jiu-jitsu--Brazil. I. Title.
  GV1114.W34 2008
  796.815'20981--dc22

                              2007034113

ISBN-10: 0-7360-7488-0
ISBN-13: 978-0-7360-7488-9

The Web addresses cited in this text were current as of August 2007.

Acquisitions Editor: Justin Klug
Senior Editor: Sarah Goulding
Managing Editor: Cory Weber
Designer: Glyn Bridgewater
Cover Designer: Keith Blomberg
Photographer (cover and interior): Mike Holdsworth
Publishing Director: Rosemary Wilkinson
Production: Marion Storz

Reproduction by Pica Digital Pte Ltd, Singapore
Printed and bound in Malaysia by Times Offset (M) Sdn Bhd

10 9 8 7 6 5 4 3 2 1

Human Kinetics
Web site: www.HumanKinetics.com

United States: Human Kinetics
P.O. Box 5076, Champaign, IL 61825-5076
800-747-4457
e-mail: humank@hkusa.com

Canada: Human Kinetics
475 Devonshire Road Unit 100, Windsor, ON N8Y 2L5
800-465-7301 (in Canada only)
e-mail: orders@hkcanada.com

DISCLAIMER

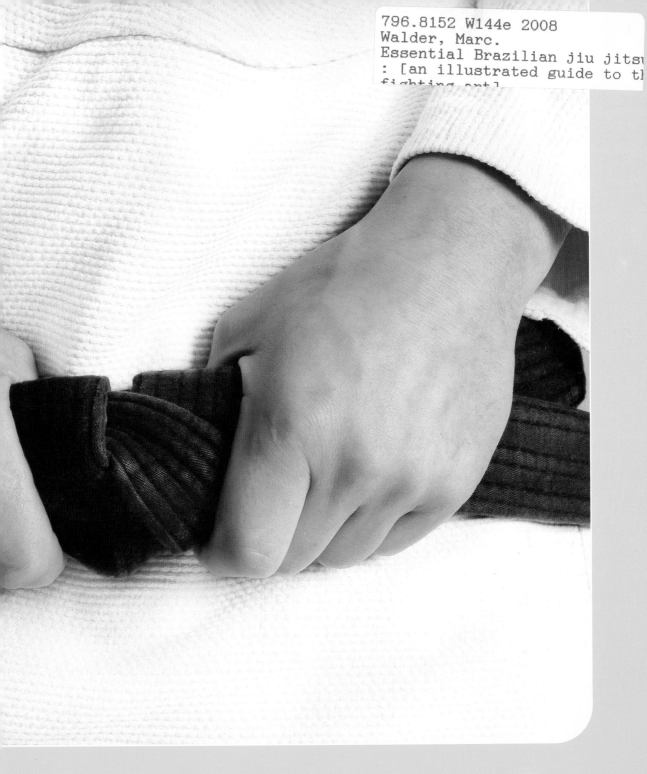

AUTHOR'S ACKNOWLEDGMENTS

I would like to give special thanks to two of the greatest men I have ever had the honor and the privilege to meet – Mr Lane B Dalley and Mestre Mauricio Motta Gomes. I would also like to thank all those who have taught me and quenched my thirst for knowledge in my search for jiu jitsu excellence. Thanks also to my family and friends for their help, patience and support. Finally, to my students past and present for their friendship and trust in allowing me to guide them to their personal goals in jiu jitsu. I hope I have had a positive influence on their lives.

CONTENTS

INTRODUCTION

Welcome to Brazilian jiu jitsu (BJJ) — an introduction and beginners' guide. The purpose of this book is to familiarize you with the techniques and structure of BJJ and to give you a basic understanding of the objectives and strategy of this martial art. No book can replace an experienced instructor, but it can be an extremely valuable reference tool and a great guide toward your development in the art of BJJ.

BJJ is very much a grappling sport. A grappler's objective in a fight is to avoid being hit and then control and submit an attacker, rather than relying solely on striking as a means of offense and defense. When facing an opponent, the grappler stays out of range of the punches and kicks, then closes the distance so he can clinch (grab hold of) the opponent and stay close to him. Staying close minimizes the effectiveness of the strikes and also takes away most of your opponent's power.

The next step for the grappler is to take the attacker down to the ground, where they will be able to control them more easily than they can in the standing position. Once on the ground the experienced grappler can manipulate and control the opponent further, and can eventually end the fight with a submission.

The advantage that a BJJ grappler has is that he can predict his opponent's moves before he makes them — people, especially those with little or no experience of grappling, are prone to making common mistakes when fighting, and with prior knowledge of the opponent's next move, BJJ fighters have the advantage and can remain one step ahead.

Although BJJ fighters have the ability to kick and punch, the submissions they have at their disposal mean that they do not have to rely on them. As a general rule, grapplers use strikes more as a means to maneuver an opponent into a vulnerable position for a submission, rather than to cause or inflict damage. Jiu jitsu is based on leverage rather than strength, and this allows you to apply as little or as much force as you want to, or deem necessary.

The origins of Brazilian jiu jitsu

Scholars of martial arts have traced the origins of jiu jitsu as far back as ancient Greece around 5,000 years ago. It is thought to have been passed on to Buddhist monks by Alexander the Great and his soldiers during their attempted conquest of Asia. Because of the monks' spiritual and moral beliefs, it is believed that they devised a system of self-defense that would allow them to defend and protect themselves without having to hurt their attacker.

Wishing to spread the teachings of Buddhism, the monks traveled from India into China, where many of them settled and established a network of temples. Buddhism became very popular with the Chinese people, and many of them became Buddhist monks themselves. Japanese scholars learned of Buddhism in China and decided to send envoys to understand its philosophy and bring their findings back to Japan. On returning home after a number of years, the Japanese envoys brought with them not just the moral and spiritual beliefs of the monks, but also their martial arts system.

Due to the effectiveness and superiority of the monks' fighting techniques, the Japanese masters integrated much of the Buddhist martial arts approach into their own martial arts systems of the era. This was undoubtedly the beginning of Japanese jiu jitsu as we know it today. As an art, jiu jitsu was thus developed over many centuries, by many different people from various cultural backgrounds.

Over the following centuries jiu jitsu became extremely popular with the Japanese people, and during its most successful period there were estimated to be around 700 different styles. Jiu jitsu originally encompassed all fighting ranges, techniques and

strategies, which including striking, pressure points, throwing and joint manipulation.

Masters of the time, however, concluded that jiu jitsu should be broken down into smaller divisions, leading to the birth of individual styles that we know of today such as karate, judo and aikido. Although jiu jitsu remained as a style, many of the lethal Samurai techniques were shared between all the other arts.

MITSUYO MAEDA, AN EARLY MASTER OF JIU JITSU.

Mitsuyo Maeda (1878–1941) studied jiu jitsu as a boy, and at the age of 18 he started studying the art of judo at the Kodokan in Tokyo. He trained there for many years under the watchful eye of the founder of judo, Jigoro Kano (1860–1938). Maeda rapidly excelled because of his childhood jiu jitsu experience. He developed very quickly in the art of judo and became one of Kano's most talented students.

In an effort to make judo more popular and possibly have it included in the Olympic Games, Kano sent two representatives from the Kodokan to the United States so that they could demonstrate the art's effectiveness to a larger audience. Maeda was one of these representatives, and he impressed the Americans with his outstanding performances during his demonstrations and challenge matches.

Maeda ended up teaching judo on the East Coast and continued to accept challenge matches for money. He was not very successful as a teacher and decided to become a professional fighter instead, earning a tough reputation as a fighter and often causing his opponents difficulty. The challenge matches led him to travel widely, including many parts of Europe and the Americas. Maeda became quite famous, even earning himself the nickname of "Count Combat," or *Conde Koma* in Brazil.

After traveling through much of South America, Maeda ended up settling in Brazil. He became very popular there and established himself in the city of Belem. It was there he began to teach once again. Maeda taught jiu jitsu and judo to the military and police as well as to local people. He had many private students and among them was a prominent Brazilian official named Gastão Gracie. The two men soon became good friends and Gastão even assisted Maeda in the establishment of a Japanese colony in Belem. After being friends for some time, Maeda offered to teach jiu jitsu to Gastão's sons, an offer that he readily accepted.

The birth of Gracie jiu jitsu

Carlos Gracie, Gastão's son, learned the basics of jiu jitsu and judo from Maeda and, after showing a natural flair, he quickly became one of his best students. Over the next few years, Carlos also taught his brothers Oswaldo, Jorge, Gastão and Hélio. Hélio was a frail, sickly boy and because of his disposition was only allowed to learn jiu jitsu visually, from the sidelines. Over the next few years, Hélio memorized all of his brother's teachings. One day when Carlos was late for a private lesson, Hélio stood in for his brother. After the lesson the student liked his teaching style so much that he asked for his private tuition to continue under Hélio.

HÉLIO GRACIE (CENTER) WITH TWO OF HIS STUDENTS, PEDRO AND GUI VALENTE.

Hélio had great difficulty in applying many of the traditional Japanese jiu jitsu techniques because of his size, illness and poor physical stature. As a result, he devised ways of adapting and changing the application of the techniques, so it was possible for them to be performed with the minimum amount of effort and to gain the maximum results. Hélio wanted the techniques to work for anybody, regardless of size, speed or strength. He eliminated techniques that could not be adapted or changed and replaced them with alternatives or more efficient moves, and so Brazilian jiu jitsu was developed.

With jiu jitsu now growing in popularity, the Gracie family decided to move to Rio de Janeiro. It was there that they carried on Maeda's tradition of challenge matches, which were open to any other style of martial art in order to prove BJJ's effectiveness in combat. As a result of the Gracie family's impressive displays and victories, BJJ became hugely popular in Brazil. During

the last century, the Gracie family issued challenges to champions of wrestling, boxing, judo, jiu jitsu, karate and kung fu so that they could demonstrate the martial superiority of BJJ.

Despite huge popularity and success in Brazil, the Gracie family and BJJ were relatively unknown to the rest of the world for a number of years. During the 1970s a few Gracie family members traveled to the United States, and it was here that many settled to make their homes and begin teaching BJJ to a wider audience, often in makeshift dojos in back rooms and garages.

The Ultimate Fighting Championship

Gracie jiu jitsu was taught to a select few who were lucky enough to hear about it by word of mouth. It was in 1993 that BJJ finally gained national and international popularity, when it was aired on US television in a show called the Ultimate Fighting Championship (UFC). Live on pay-per-view TV, the effectiveness and dominance of the Gracie-style BJJ over various other styles of martial art was shown to the world in live, no rules, reality cage fighting matches.

Up until the emergence of the UFC, many martial arts styles would not compete outside of their own disciplines or against each other in open combat. It was this that made the UFC so unique and controversial. Now people had the chance to see what would really work in a real fight, and which style would prove to be the most effective. Regardless of size, skill or speed, most matches resembled what you might see in a street fight. Skilled martial artists with previous fight experience were suddenly exposed to the reality of a real fight without rules, the confines of a ring or referee intervention. The only way the fight would end was if you gave up, were knocked unconscious or your corner threw in the towel. The UFC was the real deal, with no choreography and no second chances.

In amongst the mayhem and confusion, one fighter by the name of Royce Gracie calmly and gracefully fought his way through each round to win fight after fight with almost scientific precision and ease, winning up to four matches in a single evening. Despite his slight build and obvious weight disadvantage, Royce was victorious throughout, seemingly never under any pressure and with nothing more than a few scratches at the end. Most of the fighters were cut, exhausted and bruised. Some even had broken bones, and many went to the hospital for treatment. Spectators and the martial arts community were at a loss for words as this quiet, unassuming Brazilian fought his way through boxing, judo, wrestling and kickboxing champions, even though he was outmatched much of the time for size and strength and fighting against experienced and skilled opponents. Royce himself declared that his success was all down to the effectiveness of his family's brand of jiu jitsu. And after the initial shock and surprise, people flocked in serious numbers to learn the Brazilian style of jiu jitsu.

The merging of skills

It was now very apparent that to be a truly effective martial artist and to be able to defend yourself in a real fight situation, knowing how to grapple and fight on the ground had to become a major inclusion, along with the striking arts, when learning self-defense. For many years people assumed that it would be the strikers who were more likely to be victorious in a fight. The exposure of BJJ and the grappling arts in the Ultimate Fighting Championship smashed this theory, and highlighted the importance of cross-training.

The UFC heralded a whole new era, as fighters began to understand the importance of merging striking and grappling. A good striker who incorporated BJJ grappling techniques into his arsenal became a much more unpredictable and dangerous fighter, as did the grappler or BJJ fighter who developed his striking offense and defense. No longer was one style seen as enough to be victorious in the cage.

In the early years of the UFC, many fighters broke bones in their hands and wrists because there was no use of wraps or gloves, meaning that many fighters could not continue because of the pain and the damage inflicted. When hand wrapping and gloves were introduced, strikers could throw punches freely and as hard as they could without the fear of damaging their hands. This, combined with the use of BJJ principles, revolutionized the event.

A martial art for everyone

Although many people associate BJJ with cage fighting because of the Royce Gracie connection with the UFC, there is much more to the art than this. Although BJJ is very successful in the cage, it has been stated by the Gracie family that the UFC was merely a staging platform, used to showcase BJJ's effectiveness in a real fight situation to a wider audience.

BJJ as a martial art is arguably one of the most complete and effective fighting arts in the world today, and it is not just for those who want to fight in a professional capacity. BJJ has developed many of its techniques for self-defense and has also organized specific programs to help many police, military and law enforcement agencies around the world. Jiu jitsu techniques and strategies have been adjusted to help officers apprehend criminals more safely, without risk of harm to themselves or to those they wish to subdue. This means that BJJ is a great aid to arrest and restraint procedures, weapons control and disarmament, including sticks, knives and even firearms. BJJ is uniquely suitable for this due to the simplicity of its techniques and strategies, and the ease with which they can be incorporated into existing law enforcement training programs. The problems of today's blame culture, whereby many officers are open to allegations while carrying out their duties, are almost eliminated because of the way that jiu jitsu theory, principles and techniques can be applied. It is a similar story in many armed forces around the world, which have recognized BJJ's effectiveness and seen the importance of incorporating its techniques into their basic training programs for new recruits.

This versatile and adaptable martial art also has enormous benefits for those who wish to learn self-defense. BJJ has an extensive self-defense element, with simple and easy to use techniques that cover all aspects of a street attack, from grabs and holds to kicks and punches, and basic weapons disarmament.

Gracie jiu jitsu has also developed a specific program addressing rape prevention and awareness training for women, a self-defense program that has been invaluable to those who have participated.

BJJ is open to everyone, regardless of physical ability, age or social background. Despite its at-times controversial history in cage fighting, it is also enormous fun — many practitioners who begin training for self-defense reasons will also find the learning experience extremely enjoyable. Training can become extremely challenging but also highly rewarding, as the experience becomes about more than just learning to defend and protect yourself. BJJ can have a hugely positive effect on a student's confidence and self-esteem, as they develop and perfect their technical ability and start to see the results of their hard work. Above all, it is also a great form of physical exercise — through simple and natural training methods, muscles get stronger and flexibility and fitness levels improve as you learn to push yourself to much higher levels of personal development.

BJJ IS AN EXCELLENT MARTIAL ART TO LEARN FOR SELF-DEFENSE.

GETTING STARTED

Whether you are completely new to martial arts or you have a great deal of experience, the advice when starting Brazilian jiu jitsu remains the same: take your time, enjoy the learning process and allow yourself a realistic time frame to get to know the intricacies of the art.

Simply reading this book is not enough, as knowing and doing are two totally different concepts. To become proficient in BJJ and have a true understanding of how each technique works, it is necessary to couple your mental knowledge with physical action so that thought becomes reaction. You need to develop muscle memory, and this will only be gained and retained through physical interaction and consistent, regular practice with a partner.

Many people mistakenly rush through important information to get to certain parts or sections they may find more interesting than others. This is not recommended, as every section and technique in this or any kind of instructional book is relevant and important — it would not have been included if it wasn't. With martial arts in particular you cannot skip any part of the learning process if you truly want to excel, and to have a complete understanding of the basics you must study every section and scenario thoroughly. If you are ever uncertain about a move or technique, seek outside help or advice before proceeding.

A mistake that many new students make is to speed from one technique to the next in an effort to learn everything quickly and get to the end of the book. Always remember the importance of repetition, practicing each technique as many times as necessary in order to master it. It is better to know a few techniques extremely well than a lot of techniques improperly. It is also important to remember that the best fighters and practitioners in BJJ are extremely familiar with the basic techniques. Master the basics — they are your foundation. The professionals know that without solid basics, performing more advanced moves or competing against other high level opponents is almost impossible.

Don't become discouraged if you make errors or find it hard to perfect a technique. If you're finding something difficult, take a break, review the technique in the book, start again after a short time and remember that even the best people make mistakes. Try not to overtrain — you must give yourself time and let the information be absorbed. As you become more consistent you will gain in confidence, and your speed and timing will come naturally over time simply through repetition and constant drilling of the techniques.

Relaxation is extremely important in BJJ and yet one of the most difficult things to accomplish. Many people find that they can perform the techniques with strength and speed, but this is not the main objective — you should always be looking to refine your technical ability first. It is important, therefore, to try and relax as you practice and train. If you find yourself using strength rather than technique, you will always be beaten by more proficient, faster opponents. It is far better to develop your leverage, timing and technical knowledge. Try to feel the subtlety of the techniques and develop your sensitivity as much as you can. Strength and athletic ability are relevant, especially if you wish to compete or fight in a professional capacity, but when starting out your priority should be to develop technique first and endurance second, with strength and speed coming later.

Instead of showing individual techniques, the positions in this book have been structured in cycles so you are able to get an idea of your next step, or the choices you have. This is how they would be structured in a class environment, so hopefully this book will compliment your work in class. You should also be able to connect the moves with one another, which will help to make them easier to remember.

MOST INJURIES OCCUR AS A RESULT OF TRAINING TOO HARD OR NOT TAPPING TO A SUBMISSION — TRAIN SENSIBLY!

Safety first

As you study this book and practice the techniques, the safety of you and your training partners should be your highest priority, along with training sensibly in a safe environment. There are techniques covered in this book that, if used incorrectly, can cause pain and physical harm. Your objective when using such techniques is always to apply them carefully and slowly, so that your partner has the time and opportunity to tap (submit) and let you know when to release the hold.

Tapping physically on your partner or saying verbally to stop will prevent serious injury when you are in any kind of submission. Resisting a submission is dangerous and is not recommended. You are advised against this and do so at your own risk. The submission techniques in this book have been deliberately highlighted so that you can see where the dangers are before you practice,

and apply caution where necessary. Look for this symbol:

Submission

Introducing yourself into training slowly is sensible, especially if you are new to training or are returning after a long lay-off. If you have any doubts about your physical condition, you should seek professional medical advice before you commence any kind of physical activity or program.

It is also advisable to warm up and cool down properly before you exercise. Be sure not to neglect this area of training, as most injuries occur when the joints and muscles are cold. Cooling down and stretching after a training session will help to prevent muscle soreness following your workout, which also helps to improve recovery times.

The belt system

Before you begin learning how to do Brazilian jiu jitsu, it is useful to know a little about the hierarchy within the sport. Many people are distracted or overly concerned with the way the belt systems work in martial arts. Although belt rank can help you to see your current level and to gauge your progress, it is important not to allow thoughts of promotion through the ranks to override the development of your technique. Allow promotions to happen naturally over time as you grow in experience. You should never try to jump levels too quickly, as more often than not you will find yourself in difficulties with a more highly-skilled opponent. Only consistent training and experience in sparring will prepare you mentally and physically for the higher belt levels.

The main factors that facilitate the award of rank and belt status in BJJ are based on the following criteria:

- Consistency in attendance.
- Attitude in class, in terms of personal behavior and the treatment of your fellow students.
- Knowledge and performance of techniques while you are training.

NEVER TRY TO JUMP BELT LEVELS TOO QUICKLY — TRUST IN YOUR INSTRUCTOR TO PROMOTE YOU WHEN YOU ARE TRULY READY.

DISCIPLINE AND RESPECT ARE IMPORTANT, BUT CHILDREN SHOULD ENJOY TRAINING AND HAVE FUN.

It is important that you trust your teacher, as they will know your strengths and weaknesses. Always bear in mind that being promoted is not just about being tough, or being the best fighter. Most BJJ schools have no formal grading system and students are usually awarded a higher rank when the instructor feels that they have consistently displayed and met the necessary requirements — promotion of each student is based on individual personal circumstances and merits.

The system of promotion in BJJ has always led to high standards being maintained throughout the ranks, and competition between BJJ schools and fight teams has only served to increase belt level benchmarks even higher. The only major difference between one school and another regarding belts is the use of stripes on each belt color — the traditional BJJ belt has a small black strip where promotional stripes can be added. There are a maximum of four stripes on each student belt color up until the rank of black belt. Promotion at black belt level is awarded on a time and experience basis. Some instructors do not put much emphasis on gauging the progress between belt colors by adding stripes, although most instructors deem it an important part of the promotional process.

It is not possible to receive a blue belt in BJJ until the age of 16 years. Before this age juvenile color belts are given, and the promotion system for children is based on the same principles as it is with the adults, although the emphasis is slightly more relaxed when teaching children. Juvenile belt colors are white, yellow, orange and green, while adult colors are white, blue, purple, brown, black, black and red, and finally red.

BJJ positions

There are some basic BJJ positions that you need to be familiar with in order to understand the terminology used in this book. It is important to remember that there are may variables within BJJ and it is impossible to show them all, but the basic positions shown here will help your development and understanding of the art.

The mount (above)

A mount is a dominant offensive top position, in which you look to control your opponent and maintain the mount, while at the same time looking for a submission. The person in the bottom position is very vulnerable and will concentrate his efforts on escaping and securing a more advantageous position.

The guard (above)

Here the opponent in white has the opponent in blue in his guard, whose objective will be to protect himself from submissions, keep his balance and try to pass around his opponent's legs to a more dominant position. The person maintaining the guard will aim to make his opponent lose his balance and sweep him to gain a top position, or submit him with an armlock or a choke.

The headlock (above)

The fighter in blue is holding his opponent in a head-lock, and although he cannot cause him too many problems, he can control him very easily if the opponent in white does not understand how to defend or escape from this position. The person in the headlock would look to make himself safe by positioning himself correctly and escape by reversing the situation to his advantage.

The sweep/reversal (above)

A sweep or reversal is any situation in which a person moves from a bottom position to a top one, while maintaining control of the opponent. The top position is very favorable, giving you the advantages of weight and gravity over your opponent.

The cross-side (above)

This movement is best seen from above. The fighter in white is clearly controlling his opponent from the top and can use his whole body weight, which can make it difficult for his opponent to move. The person maintaining the cross-side would look to control and maintain his position, look for a submission or advance to the mount.

BASIC MOVEMENTS

Now that you are familiar with the basic positions in BJJ, you can begin to incorporate them into movements. Practice the exercises that follow as many times as you need to in order to master them — they will form the basis of everything else you do in BJJ.

Stand in base

It is important not to underestimate the importance of standing up correctly from a seated position on the ground. This particular technique is connected to many other situations in BJJ and they will become apparent as your level advances. The two main aspects to remember while getting to your feet in a fight or confrontation are balance and having the correct defensive posture. This will prevent you from being pushed back to the ground and also protects you from being hit as you get up. Once you familiarize yourself with the movement, repeat it a set number of times on both sides as part of a warm-up before you begin your training session.

A Sit with both legs bent, one knee up and one knee flat against the floor. Rest one hand on the ground slightly behind you, with your elbow resting on your raised knee.

B Distributing the weight evenly between the supporting hand and foot, lift your hips slightly so that you can pivot your other leg under your body.
(Continued)

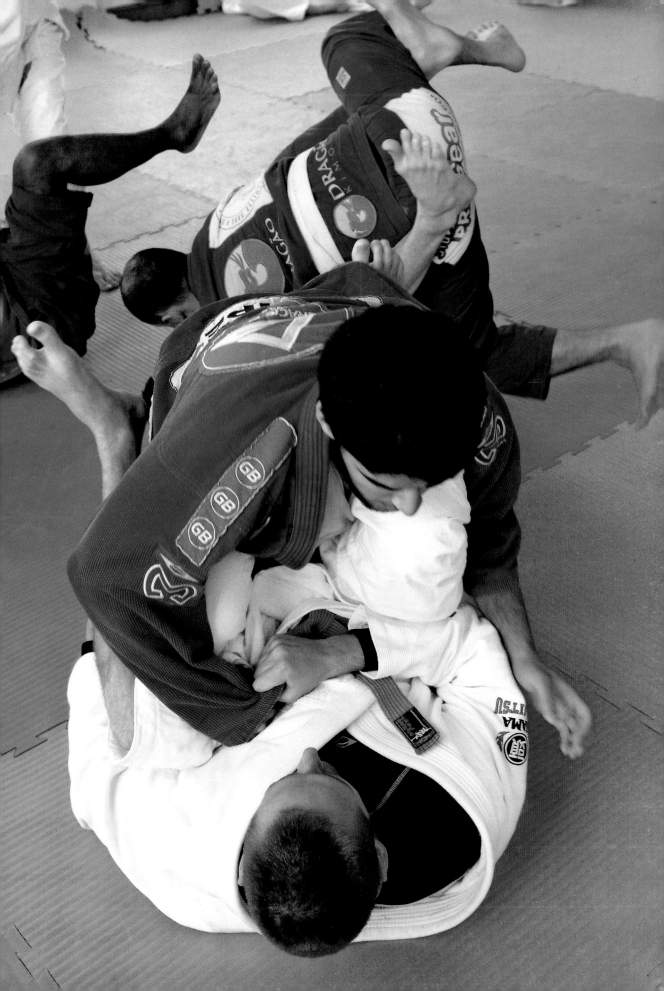

(Continued)

C   Place your right foot on the ground next to your hand. Now that the foot is placed firmly on the ground, you can continue to a standing position.

D   Make sure that your standing position is firm and solid, with good balance and posture.

Bridge escape

In this drill, the idea is to simulate reversing your opponent when he is mounted on top of you. This drill will familiarize your muscles and reflexes to the mechanics of the movement without having the weight of another person on top of you. This is also a great warm-up drill and can be done on both sides.

A   Start flat on your back, making sure to keep your arms close to your body. Bring your feet close to your hips.

B   Choosing a side, raise your hips up as high as you can by driving off your feet, then start bridging over your shoulder.

C   Continue bridging over your shoulder and move forward onto your knees, making sure they are wide apart for balance.

D   To finish, move upright and sit back in a squatting position onto your heels.

Elbow escape

It is important when practicing this drill to keep your arms close to your body and avoid extending them. The reason for this is partly that it requires a great deal of strength to push an opponent off you, but primarily because you will leave yourself open to being submitted in various types of armlock. Again, this technique can be used as a great warm-up once you are familiar with it and can perform the movement smoothly.

A Lie on the floor with your left knee bent and your foot flat on the ground. Lift your hips slightly by distributing your weight onto your foot and your shoulder.

B Keeping your right leg extended, push off from your left foot and move your hips in a backward motion.

C Swivel onto your right side, keeping your right leg extended, and move your hands down toward your feet

D Bring your right knee up to your chest and extend your arms, to mimic bracing yourself against an opponent.

E Move your left shoulder back flat to the floor. Bring your body back to the starting position and repeat the movement on the opposite side.

Bridge escape with partner

Now we can see how the bridge escape works with a partner mounted on top. When someone is mounted on you, one of the most important things to remember is to keep your arms close to your body at all times. One of the first moves you can try in this situation is to bridge your opponent off, thereby sweeping and reversing him so that you end up in the top position.

A The partner on top is trying to choke his opponent's neck. As the bottom partner, you should take advantage of this by holding his wrist and elbow, while also trapping the foot on the same side as you are holding the elbow.

i Note the position and grips that the bottom partner uses to control the attacker's arm.

ii Note also the position of the bottom partner's foot.

B As the bottom partner, start off the move by driving your hips upward as high as you can. Continue bridging over your shoulder and onto your knees.

C As your opponent falls, follow him to come over onto the top position, ending up in the guard.

(Continued)

B

ii

C

(Continued)

D   Making sure not to lose your balance, widen your knees and sit back a little.

E   Finish blocking your opponent's bicep and position your other arm on the opposite leg, ready to pass the guard.

Elbow escape with partner

The elbow and hip escapes are the most effective movements you will learn in Brazilian jiu jitsu. If you cannot bridge off the person who is on top and you have no choice but to be on your back in a fight, the best place to have the opponent is inside your guard. The reason you are relatively safe when you have your opponent in your guard is because you have a certain amount of control over him with your legs. You will also be sensitive to his movements and have some degree of command over his balance. The guard is also used as a starting point to mount many of your attacks and reversals once you have secured your position defensively. The elbow escape should be used when your opponent is mounted on you, has a wide base and is not holding or choking you.

A Your opponent is mounted on you but is not choking or holding you. Note that the bottom partner's starting position is exactly the same as it is during the elbow escape drill on pages 24—25.

Any time your opponent tries to hold you or choke you from the mounted position, this will give you the opportunity to execute a bridge escape (see pages 26—28). In a situation where your opponent does not do this, you should use an elbow escape.

B Brace the inside of your opponent's knee and block his hip. Pushing off from your right foot will then drive the hips in a backward direction, also bringing your knee out toward your chest.

C Release your foot and bring it out by circling it around and then back inside your opponent's leg. Continue your escape by bracing your shoulder and your opposite knee.

(Continued)

(Continued)

D   Bring your knee up toward your chest and free your other leg, turning toward your opponent and trapping him inside your guard in the process.

E   Bring your left leg up toward your chest by putting your weight on your right foot, and move your hips backward so that you can free your leg.

F   You should now be able to finish the sequence. Cross your ankles and close the guard around your opponent's waist.

Elbow escape variation

As you improve and develop your skill level, you will find that situations change from moment to moment. The reason for this is that you are in live practice against a resistant partner. During a fight, things do not always happen the way we want or plan them to, and the situation can change very quickly. The following technique shows an example of starting from the mounted position as before, but with a partner who is heavy or putting all his weight on you, which limits the space in which you have to escape.

A   As the bottom partner, you have been mounted and pinned by your opponent. Be sure to keep your elbows in and one leg flat. Turn your hips as much as you can toward the leg that is flat on the ground.

B   Using the leg that is on the ground, drive your knee outward to push open your opponent's leg and expose his ankle. Reach over with your other leg and hook your toes under the ankle.

(Continued)

(Continued)

C Use your elbow and foot, and at the same time lift your opponent's leg slightly so that you can slide your leg under and out.

D With your free leg inside your opponent's, you can now continue your escape, planting your left foot firmly while turning to face the opposite side.

i In the reverse angle, you can clearly see the continuation of the escape.

E Plant the right foot firmly and move your hips backward so that you can free your other leg.

F Now that your opponent is inside your legs, you can close the guard to finish the movement.

33

Connecting movements together

The eventual objective as you progress and gain a higher level of skill is to link the movements and techniques together. Initially, though, you must learn them individually so that you understand them and are confident in performing the mechanics of the movements, remembering the specific details of each technique. Always bear in mind, however, that when you are training against a non-compliant opponent, the situation is always subject to change and can become difficult. Combining techniques together will make your execution of them easier to perform against higher-level opponents.

In this sequence you should start to bridge your opponent off as before, but the situation will change during your escape.

A Your opponent is mounted on top of you. Hold your opponent's wrist and elbow and trap his foot, with the intention of raising your hips to roll to your knees onto the top position.

B As you raise your hips, your opponent counters by posting his leg (stretching it out) so that he does not lose his balance and fall.

C Because your opponent is posting his leg, this allows you the space to switch into the elbow escape. Do this by keeping your hips raised, then bracing the right knee to retain the space. Allow your left knee to come up to your chest.

D Bring your left leg up and over your opponent's and rest your calf on your opponent's thigh. (Continued)

(Continued)

E   Continue your escape and turn to face the opposite side by bracing his shoulder and the opposite knee, bringing your right knee up so that your leg can escape.

F   Move your hips backward so that you can free your leg. This will allow you to finish the move by crossing your ankles around your opponent's waist.

Passing the guard

Passing the guard can be one of the most testing situations in grappling, but it is especially so in BJJ. One of the main reasons for this is that the offensive and defensive techniques and strategies involve the use of the legs. The basic pass that you learn in this book will not be the final one you end up using, but you have to have a starting point and a good frame of reference that will teach you the correct posture, grips, balance and alignment for passing the guard. As your level and understanding improves, you will automatically choose an advanced pass that suits your jiu jitsu game and style. Getting the fundamentals of the basic pass correct in the beginning, however, will save a great deal of frustration at a later stage.

Basic kneeling pass

A   Start off on top, inside your opponent's guard. Keep a good posture by sitting upright with your back straight, your knees open for balance and your hand on your opponent's bicep.

B   Move your left leg up and turn your body in the same direction. This will open up space for your hand to pass inside and control your opponent's leg.

(Continued)

(Continued)

C   Open the guard and bring your opponent's leg onto your shoulder. Reach forward to grasp the opposite collar and change your base by switching the position of your legs and continually driving the weight forward.

i   Note how deep the grip on the collar is, and the position of the hand.

D   Transfer all of your weight forward, driving your opponent's knee toward his head.

E   Relax your body weight down, arch your back slightly and drive your hips toward the ground, before passing your body around the leg.

F   Finally you should end up in the cross-side position, with your chest and bodyweight pinning your opponent flat on his back.

Basic standing pass

As you practice and become familiar with the basic pass, you will gain confidence with your posture, balance and grips. This will allow you to try other types of passes, and one that is also very useful to practice is the basic standing pass. This is more or less the same as the basic pass from the knees, but because you are standing up you have to make some technical adjustments to allow for the slight differences.

A   Begin this sequence with your strongest hand on top, maintaining good posture and balance and taking your time to get the correct grips.

i   With your strongest hand, grip both lapels. Your other hand should take a slightly lower grip.

B   Stand up, maintaining your balance and posture. Make sure that the first step you take is the with leg on the same side as the stonger hand you are gripping with.

ii   Note the position that your knee and elbow should be in.

C   Standing in a solid stance, make sure that your hips are pressing forward and that your knee and elbow are together. Let go with your other hand to make a downward pressure to open the legs.

(Continued)

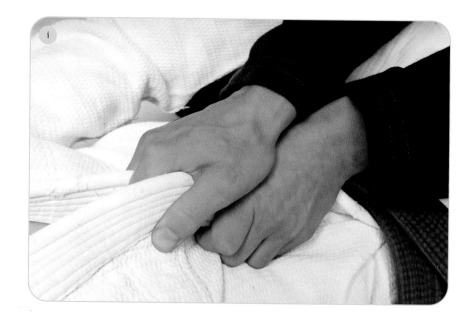

(Continued)

D From this angle we can see that once the legs are open, you should push your opponent's knee to the ground, sliding your knee through and over the top and pinning your opponent's leg to the ground.

iii Your foot should be hooked over your opponent's knee, trapping the leg.

E Reaching forward under your opponent's shoulder, transfer your base at the same time by stepping backward and sitting back. Control your opponent's knee and delay taking your foot away from his leg until you are ready to complete the pass.

iv Note from this top view the hand and foot positions that you should have achieved.

F Finally, switch to the cross-side position by removing your foot and switching your base again.

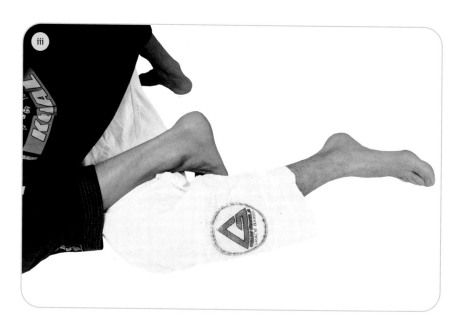

MAINTAINING THE TOP POSITION

When you pass the guard to the cross-body position, the first objective is to control the opponent to limit his chances of escape. Once you have established control, one of your options is to look for and apply a submission. Another is to move into the mounted position. If you have difficulty in submitting your opponent from the cross-side, your next option should then be to mount.

The importance of the mount

Like the cross-side, when you reach the mount position you have the ability to control, dominate, tire and submit your opponent. There are many ways you can submit your opponent from the cross-side, and in the next few techniques we will look at some of the basic submissions available before looking at some basic ways that you can mount your opponent. How you mount is a personal preference, and will also be subject to your level and ability. Many beginners are apprehensive when attempting to mount, through fear of the opponent escaping, reversing or sweeping them. Although this fear is natural and everybody experiences it, your intention should always be to advance and improve your situation, or finish the fight with a submission.

Submission

Figure-four keylock from the cross-side position

A keylock involves holding the forearm and using it to apply torque to the shoulder as if it were a key in a keyhole. It can be applied from a multitude of positions and is a submission hold that you should master. "Figure-four" refers to the wrist hold used here, which creates a shape like the figure four.

A   Begin in a cross-side position on top of your opponent, who has left his arm open for attack.

B   Maintain your position by keeping your chest and body weight on your opponent. Bring your elbow tight to your opponent's neck and control his wrist. (Continued)

(Continued)

C Reach under your opponent's elbow and hold your own wrist.

i This is how the grip on your own wrist should look. Note that there is no use of the thumbs in this particular grip.

D To apply the lock, bring your head down to your hands and slide your opponent's wrist along the ground. At the same time, lift the elbow up until your opponent taps.

Submission

Kimura from the cross-side position

The Kimura is a reverse keylock that puts pressure on your opponent's shoulder joint and, depending on the angle, the elbow joint as well. It is named after Masahiko Kimura, who used it to defeat one of the founders of BJJ, Hélio Gracie.

A   Begin in a cross-side position on top of your opponent, who has left his arm open for attack.

B   Control your opponent's wrist with your right hand, keeping your elbow tight against his body.

C   Reaching under your opponent's arm with your left hand, grab hold of your own wrist.

(Continued)

(Continued)

i   From this top view, we can see how you should have switched your hip position in order to subdue your opponent.

D   Lean your weight forward and step your leg over your opponent's head. If needed, move your weight back in order to create a solid base.

E   To apply the Kimura, bring your opponent's shoulder off the ground slightly and drive his wrist toward his head until he taps.

Armlock from the cross-side

An armlock is a joint lock that hyperextends the elbow joint and is one of the most common ways to achieve a submission. Administering an armlock involves using your whole body as a lever while preventing your opponent from escaping. This means that they are more easily performed from a dominant grappling position on the ground. You should always perform armlocks in a slow and controlled manner, so that your opponent has plenty of opportunity to tap out before any damage is inflicted.

A   Begin in a cross-side position. Here, your opponent has his arm across your shoulder.

B   Open your collar with one hand and reach underneath your opponent's arm with your other hand, grasping your collar to trap his arm with your grip.

i   One hand should be helping the other to secure the grip.

(Continued)

Submission

(Continued)

C   From this reverse angle, we can see that your right hand should then be placed on the ground in front of your opponent's hip. You should then start to "walk" around the head to the opposite side.

D   Once you are round the other side, push your opponent onto his side and place your hand in front of his face.

E   Jump to your feet in a crouching position, with one knee on your opponent's ribs and your other foot next to your hand.

F   To finish the armlock, sit down and clamp your knees tightly together.

G   Control your opponent's wrist, then lie backward and raise your hips to apply pressure until your opponent taps.

Step-over to mount

This technique is shown from above so that you can see the details more clearly.

A   Begin this technique on top of your opponent in the cross-body position. Note the correct positioning shown here — you should have your chest directly over your opponent's for maximum control.

B   Rotate your hips and switch your leg positions, stepping one leg back for balance and keeping your other knee close to your opponent's hip. At the same time, block your opponent's knees with your arm to keep the space for you to step your leg over him.

C Step your leg all the way to the opposite side, making sure that your foot lands flat onto the ground. Be sure to land your foot and then your knee, so that you do not hurt your knee.

D You should now be ready to transfer your weight onto your hands and knees in the mounted position. Make sure you spread your arms wide to create a solid base.

Knee-over to mount

This is a similar technique to the previous one, but the idea here is to stay low and tight. Again it is shown from the top for clarity.

A   Begin this technique on top and in the cross-body position. Keep your hips low, with one leg stretched out to create a solid base and the other bent, with the knee close to the hips.

B   Staying as low and as tight as possible, slide your knee over your opponent's stomach/belt line, making sure to bring your trailing leg with you as you transfer to the mount position.

C   Transfer your weight to a central position above your opponent.

D   End in the mounted position, spreading your arms wide for stability.

Stabilizing the mount

When you have reached the mounted position it is important that you try to maintain and stabilize your position, then control your opponent before you try a submission. Many people try to submit their opponents without having the proper control, and end up being reversed or giving their opponent an opportunity to escape. If your opponent is inexperienced, it is likely that he will try to escape in predictable ways. He will also often tire himself out and make typical mistakes in his efforts to escape. When this happens, you should be ready to capitalize on it. Some of the most common situations and how to deal with them will be looked at in the next few techniques. Although they are talked about individually, you will eventually use and combine them all together.

Scenario 1: "Swim" arms

A   In this scenario you are mounted on your opponent, who is trying to push you off. Relax your weight as much as you can to make yourself as heavy as possible, then start to turn your shoulders.

B   Slide your right hand in between your opponent's arms and then place it directly onto the floor for balance. At the same time, turn your shoulders in the other direction in preparation for your other hand coming through.

C   Now you can "swim" your left hand through to the ground. Every time your opponent attempts to push on your chest, simply repeat steps A to C as many times as necessary.

Scenario 2: Opponent pushes knee

A   In this scenario you are mounted on your opponent, who is pushing your knee in an attempt to escape.
Cup the wrist that is pushing on your knee and place
your other hand on the floor.

i   Note that the thumb is not used in this
particular grip.

B   Lift your opponent's wrist up toward your own
armpit, then slide your knee forward into the space
under his arm.

(Continued)

(Continued)

C   As we can see from this reverse angle, the opponent may then switch and push on your other knee.

D   To counter this, repeat steps A and B and slide your other knee forward to end up in a high mount on your opponent's chest.

Scenario 3: Opponent pushes hips

A   You are mounted on your opponent, who simply tries to push on your hips with both hands to escape. If you resist or try to fight it, you may get thrown from the mount.

B   Sit upright and drive your hips forward. Cup your hands in readiness to clear your opponent's arms away from your hips.

C   Use of the heel of your hand and no thumb to clear your opponent's grip.

(Continued)

(Continued)

D Placing your hand on your opponent's wrist, turn your shoulder and drive your arm across your body to clear away your opponent's arm.

E Repeating the same movement on the opposite side, you can now start to put your weight forward to prevent your opponent pushing your hips again.

F Ideally you would now collapse all of your weight forward, trapping your opponent's arms and making it difficult for him to move.

Scenario 4: Opponent rolls onto stomach

A Again you are mounted on your opponent, who this time will roll onto his stomach in an attempt to escape. The best thing to do in this situation is to let your opponent turn away from you — this will expose his neck to a choke.

B Allow your opponent to turn by opening your knee slightly, maintaining your position above him. Make sure to keep your chest close to your opponent, opening your arms wide to create a solid base.

C Allow your opponent to turn onto his stomach, as this can lead to various attack options. If he changes his mind and rolls in the opposite direction, open your other knee and follow him to maintain the top position.

Scenario 5: Opponent grabs material

The main difference between this technique and the swim arms scenario (see page 56) is that your opponent grabs onto your jacket or clothing when trying to push you off. This will make it difficult for you to swim your arms through, so we have to modify the defense a little. Staying relaxed and keeping your weight heavy while maintaining your balance is a key component to staying mounted on your opponent.

Also important to remember is to take your time and not rush for a submission. Otherwise, you may lose the position completely.

A   You are mounted on your opponent, who has grabbed your jacket with both hands and is attempting to push you off to the side.

i   Your opponent's grip means that it is difficult to swim the arms through as shown previously.

B   Relax your weight and place your hand behind your opponent's neck, so that you have an anchor. Use your other hand to make a wide, stable base.

C   If your opponent tries to push you to the other side, simply repeat step B and he will be unable to gain control.

B

C

ATTACK & DEFENSE

Now you have maintained your position successfully, you can mount your offense further by attempting to submit your opponent. There are a number of ways you can do this, and in this section we will look at a few basic techniques to give you some options.

Attacks from the mount

Many people are reluctant to attack from the mount through fear of losing their position — either by being put into the guard or being reversed. It is important to maintain your position when you initiate your attacks.

Submission

Straight armlock from mount

One of the most common submissions you will encounter is the straight armlock. People with little or no grappling experience tend to push a great deal when they are trapped and trying to escape from the bottom position, and this exposes their arms and makes them vulnerable to being submitted.

A If your opponent is trying to escape from the bottom position by grabbing your collar, he will then try to push on your chest to throw you off. Place both your hands on your opponent's chest, making sure that one arm is over the top of your opponent's arm and one arm is underneath.

i This is how your arms should look (dark green material) — one arm under and one arm over your opponent's.

(Continued)

(Continued)

B Lean forward, putting as much weight on your hands as possible. Jump your feet forward so that they are in line with your opponent's shoulders.

C Keeping your weight centered on your hands, rotate yourself around and at the same time pass your leg over your opponent's head, so that you end up sideways to your opponent.

The leg you pass over your opponent's head should be on the same side as the hand in front.

D Sit down close to your opponent's shoulder, holding his wrist with both hands and keeping it close to your chest.

ii This grip detail shows the position in which your hands should be.

E Lying backward, apply pressure on the elbow joint by keeping your knees together, raising your hips upward and pulling down on the arm until your opponent taps.

Submission

Cross-choke from mount

The cross-choke is one of the most efficient moves in jiu jitsu. Many people underestimate its effectiveness, and it is often overlooked because of its simplicity. All chokes are dependent on correct application, but correctly applied it is one of the best fundamental moves you can make.

A Mounted on your opponent, open his collar with one hand and pass your other hand deep into the collar.

i Make sure that you place four fingers inside the collar and grip with your thumb.

B Now pass your other hand under the first hand and into the opposite collar, again placing four fingers inside.

ii To get a deeper bite, grip both collars and lift the shoulders slightly, then shoot both hands in as deep as you can at the same time.

C To start to apply the choke, turn your wrists so that your palms are facing toward your chest, then lower your chest down to your opponent's. Keep your elbows close to your body and expand your chest, while at the same time pulling your elbows backward until your opponent taps.

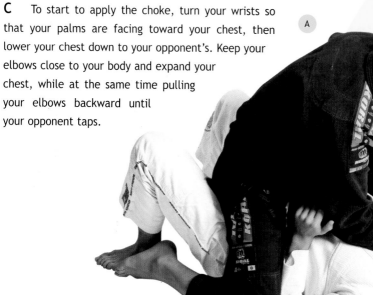

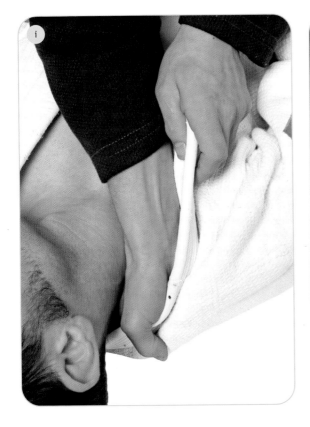

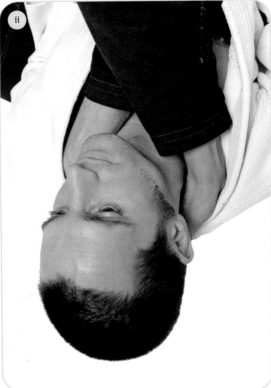

Submission

Figure-four keylock from mount

This is another very basic move with a simple concept and set-up. This technique can be extremely effective, especially if your opponent does not know the counter-move to escape.

A　Your opponent (in the bottom position) is not trying to push you off and is keeping his hands close to his neck to try to prevent the choke.

B　Place one hand on your opponent's wrist and one hand on his elbow.

C　Keeping your hands in place, lean your weight forward to pin your opponent's arm to the floor.

i　From this angle we can clearly see how you need to tuck your elbow right in to your opponent's neck. Pass your other hand under your opponent's elbow and grip your own wrist to make the figure-four lock.

D　To apply pressure to the lock, put your head on your hands and then slide your opponent's wrist along the ground toward your knee. Lift the elbow at the same time to fully apply the pressure, until your opponent taps.

A

i

Defending from the bottom

One of the keys to defending from the cross-side in the bottom position is knowing where you should put your arms, and how you should position your body correctly in relation to your opponent.

Starting correctly will ensure that you are not being totally controlled by your opponent. It will also restrict his mount attempts and limit his submission attempts. Having the knowledge and awareness of what your opponent is trying to do will allow you to be ready and correctly positioned with your body and your arms. If you are properly prepared, this will allow you to escape when the right moment presents itself.

Until you are confident and are advanced enough with your technique, patience will be one of your biggest assets. I have already mentioned that the mistake many beginners make is to try to push their opponent off when they are trapped in the bottom position on their back. By doing this, you leave yourself open to being submitted in an armlock by the person in the top position. You may have to wait for the correct time to escape, as opposed to escaping when you would like to, especially if your opponent has a higher level of skill or is much heavier than you are. In this section, we will look at various ways of defending effectively from the bottom position.

Defending the step-over mount

This is a great technique to use when you are preparing to escape from underneath your opponent. The initial set-up of your arm positioning and your body in relation to your opponent are the keys to escaping — you should be ready and waiting for the correct time to execute your escape.

A   Here, your opponent (in white) is preparing to step-over to mount (see pages 52—53). Position yourself correctly by bringing both knees up with your feet still flat on the ground. Place one hand on your opponent's hip and the other arm deep under your opponent's arm.

i   This is how your arms should look, wrapped either way around your opponent's torso.

B   As your opponent makes the step to mount, this is the correct time for you to make your move.

C   Raise your hips as high as you can, while at the same time driving your arm up under your opponent's arm to take him backward.

D   Take your opponent all the way onto his back, ending up in the top position in the guard. Make sure you maintain your posture and balance.

Defending the knee-over mount

Knowing and understanding what man-euvers your opponent will attempt will help you to understand how to set yourself up correctly for your escape. Here your opponent attempts to modify his mount attack by stay-ing low and tight so that you have to change your escape tech-nique. Patience and choosing the correct time to escape are the keys to making it feel easy.

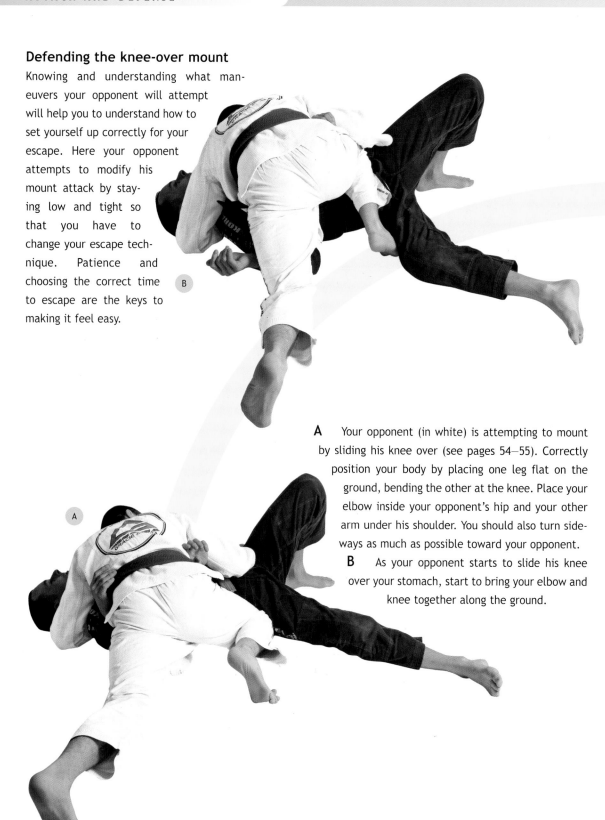

A   Your opponent (in white) is attempting to mount by sliding his knee over (see pages 54—55). Correctly position your body by placing one leg flat on the ground, bending the other at the knee. Place your elbow inside your opponent's hip and your other arm under his shoulder. You should also turn side-ways as much as possible toward your opponent.

B   As your opponent starts to slide his knee over your stomach, start to bring your elbow and knee together along the ground.

C As your opponent's weight transfers to the other side, his trailing leg will become light. This allows you to lift it slightly with your elbow and bring your right leg under and out.

D Wrap your leg around the outside of your opponent's leg.

(Continued)

(Continued)

E   Now turn to face the opposite side, bracing his shoulder and knee in preparation for freeing your other leg.

F   In this reverse angle, we can see that you should be putting your weight on your foot and lifting your hips slightly. You should then move your hips backward, bringing your knee under and out to your chest.

G   You can now finish off the move by placing your foot on the ground and moving your hips backward to free your other leg.

H   Always finish by crossing your feet and closing the guard.

Attacking from the bottom

When you find yourself on your back in a fight, your first priority, especially as a beginner, is to try to put yourself in a position where you are out of danger. The guard is one of the safest and most frequently used positions by jiu jitsu practitioners, especially if the opponent is on top and trying to punch you.

The importance of the guard position

Defensively it will be much harder for your opponent to punch, control or submit you when he is in your guard with your legs around his waist. This is because it is difficult for your opponent to mount any kind of attack, as he must pass around your legs first.

Also, offensively you have many attacking options such as armlocks, chokes and sweeps/reversals from the guard, which will distract your opponent and slow him down.

You may be in a situation where you have no choice but to be on the bottom position in a fight and you have to rely on the guard for defense. This could be for a number of reasons, for example you become tired during the fight, you have made a mistake or your opponent is bigger, heavier and stronger than you are. Trying to pass the guard can be very frustrating and tiring for your opponent, which can lead him to make critical errors which you can take advantage of. As you become more familiar and advanced with the guard position, you will find that you are able to reverse or submit your opponent from your back from a seemingly inferior position.

Submission

Kimura attack from the guard position

This technique helps you to make the most of being in the bottom position, and can be used when your opponent's arms are spread on the floor in a stable position.

A   Your opponent (in white) is in your guard and his hands are on the ground for balance. You can take

advantage of this by attacking one of his arms with the Kimura lock.

B Hold your opponent's wrist, then uncross your feet and place them on the ground so that you can slide away slightly to enable you to sit up easily.

C Sit up and reach over the top of your opponent's shoulder and under his elbow to hold your own wrist. This secures your opponent's arm in a figure-four lock.

i A close-up of the grip you should have.

(Continued)

(Continued)

D Make sure you keep your opponent's arm close to your chest then lie back, bringing your opponent down with you. At the same time, put your foot inside your opponent's leg. You now need to move yourself out from underneath your opponent and onto your side. Do this by putting your weight on your foot (left in this case) and moving your shoulder away. You may need to move your hips and shoulder again to get the correct angle to apply the finishing hold.

E Finally, cross your feet to prevent your opponent from escaping. To apply the lock, keep your opponent's arm close to your chest then drive his wrist between the two of you toward the ground.

Submission

Guillotine from the guard position

We start here from move B from the previous technique. You are about to sit up to reach over your opponent's shoulder for the Kimura lock. If your opponent anticipates this he will hide his arm, and instead of attempting the Kimura attack you should then attempt a guillotine.

A Forget about trying to secure your opponent's wrist and place your hand on the ground behind you for balance.

i Your other arm should be resting across the back of your opponent's neck, as shown here in close-up.

(Continued)

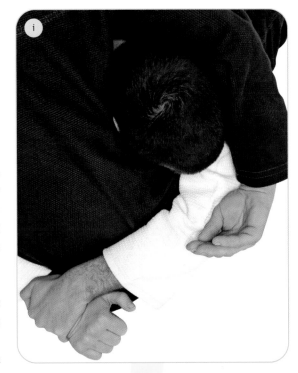

(Continued)

B   Put your weight on the hand that is placed on the ground and slide your hips away to create a space for your left hand to slide under and around your opponent's neck.

C   Now sitting up comfortably, you should be able to reach in with the hand that was on the ground and hold the wrist of the hand that is under and around your opponent's neck — this is what the grip should look like.

D   Take out any slack that is remaining in your arms to make a tighter grip around your opponent's neck, and then cross your feet to close the guard. Lie backward and to finish the choke make sure your ankles are crossed. To apply pressure on the neck, straighten your legs, pushing your opponent away. At the same time bring your hands up toward your chin until your opponent taps.

Sweep-reversal from the guard position

Being able to switch from one technique to another as you advance will allow a more free-flowing style. Your ability to unbalance your opponent can be crucial in gaining an advantage. Sometimes your opponent compromises his base or balance in an attempt to avoid a submission, which can allow you to sweep him and come to the top position, gaining a crucial advantage.

A   Your opponent is inside your guard, but this time hides both his arm and his neck by tucking his chin down to his chest.

B   Reach your arm back over to the opposite side to control your opponent's shoulder and elbow. Rest your knee on the ground and pull your opponent's arm tight to your body in preparation for your sweep/reversal.

C   Push off from your hand and foot to drive your hips upward into your opponent's chest. Raise your hips as high as possible.

(Continued)

(Continued)

D Continue to drive up and over to the side on which you are holding your opponent's elbow.

E You should end up on top in the mounted position.

Attacks — variations and combinations

Before you can link sweeps, chokes and armlocks together successfully, you must take the time to learn the basic techniques and movements individually. Otherwise your confidence and ability will not allow you to perform high-level technical sequences and combinations successfully. You should repeat each individual technique as many times as possible, making sure that you have absorbed all of the details within the technique. When you have mastered the basics you will have the ability to start to link two or more moves together, and you should be able to combine the sweeps and finishing holds successfully. Always remember that it is far better to know a small number of techniques perfectly than be able to perform a large number at a mediocre standard.

A

Submission

Armlock from the guard position

The armlock can be performed from a number of positions, although probably one of the most common is from the guard, as shown here.

A Your opponent (in white) is in your guard and steps his leg up to pass the guard. Control the arm behind your opponent's elbow and make a deep grip inside his collar.

B Because your opponent has his leg up, you are able to take advantage of the situation. Release the collar and, with the same hand, hold the inside of your opponent's ankle.

(Continued)

B

(Continued)

i   Hook your hand inside your opponent's leg as shown here.

C   Open your guard, place your foot on the ground to correctly position yourself, and then lift your hips and shoulders to arch your back as if you were performing an abdominal crunch. By turning your body to the side you can then bring your head toward your opponent's ankle.

D   Now in position, reach your leg up and over your opponent's neck and your other leg over his back. Making sure not to let go of the grip on the elbow, let go of your opponent's ankle and control his wrist.

E   To apply pressure on the armlock, make your feet heavy by pushing them toward the ground. At the same time, raise your hips and pull your opponent's wrist toward your chest until he taps.

Cross-choke from
inside the guard position

As with most of the techniques you will learn in jiu jitsu, you will find that they can all be performed in a variety of different ways from a number of different positions. Although some of the details may change slightly, the basic concepts and principles will remain the same.

A Start with your opponent in the guard, holding behind his elbow and gripping your other hand deep inside your opponent's collar.

B Release your grip on your opponent's elbow and make a circular motion with your wrist in order to come underneath your opponent's arm.

C Turn your body slightly sideways and push your other hand as deeply into your opponent's collar as possible.

D Grip the collar to take out any slack, then turn your wrists so your palms are facing your chest. You should then pull your opponent's head down to your chest using your arms and legs at the same time. (Continued)

(Continued)

i–iii Here you can see clearly how your wrists should look as they turn (imagine they are gripping the collar).

E Finish the choke by expanding your chest and shoulders and pulling your elbows toward the ground until your opponent taps.

Submission

Triangle from the guard position

The triangle is one of the most commonly known submissions in BJJ and is extremely effective. It will also become integral to your arsenal of guard techniques.

A Your opponent (in blue) is in your guard and is attempting to pass his arm under your leg to pass your guard.

(Continued)

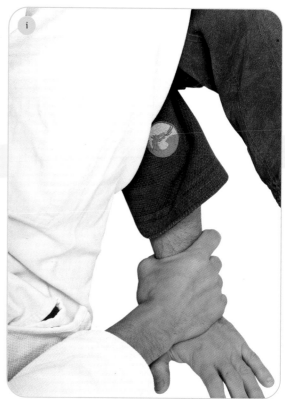

(Continued)

B   To delay your opponent's pass and give you time to set up the triangle, hold your opponent's wrist, then uncross your feet and place your free leg on the ground.

i   This is the grip you should have on your opponent's wrist.

C   Lift your shoulders slightly and use the foot on the ground to move your body toward the wrist. You should then raise your leg over your opponent's neck.

D   Reach up with your other leg, bringing it over the top of the ankle of the first leg and locking it. You are now in position for the triangle.

E   To apply pressure, hold the back of your opponent's neck with both hands and pull his head downward, while raising your hips up. Maintain the pressure until your opponent taps.

Offense from your back

As we talked about earlier, reversing or sweeping your opponent can be very advantageous when you are fighting from the guard. More often than not, in an attempt to avoid one attack, your opponent will leave an opening somewhere else that you can capitalize on.

Scissor sweep from the guard position: 1

This particular sweep is very basic and easy to learn. It can be used to test your opponent's base and to set up a secondary attack.

A You have your opponent (in black) in your guard and you are holding his arm and collar. Your opponent starts to pass, but before he can reach his hand inside your leg, open your guard and place your leg on your opponent's thigh. Use this as a pivoting point to move your hips away, so that you can position yourself on your side and can put your other leg on the ground.

C

D

B   Now in position, slide your knee across your opponent's chest and hook your foot on his hip. You can then bring your opponent forward by arching backward and pulling on his arm and collar.

C   Make a scissor motion with your legs by kicking your bottom leg under your opponent and kicking your top leg in the opposite direction.

D   As your opponent falls to the side, use the momentum to follow him over. You will end up on top in the mount position.

Scissor sweep from the guard position: 2

While you are trying to execute the scissor sweep, your opponent can sit down in a low base so as not to fall. When this happens, you need to change your leg position slightly to allow you to finish the sweep.

A   As in step A of the previous technique, your opponent is in your guard and you are holding his arm and collar as he starts to pass. This time your opponent sits low, to avoid the sweep. Place your foot on your opponent's knee.

B   To sweep, bring your opponent forward by arching backward, pulling on his arm and collar. At the same time, push his knee with your foot in the opposite direction.

C   As before, use the momentum of your opponent falling to swing around and follow him, ending up in the mount position.

D   You can now attempt to finish with a choke or an armlock because of your position and grips.

D

C

97

Headlocks

Headlocks are one of the most common forms of aggression in a street fight. Many martial arts teach various techniques using a headlock as a means of attack. Although it is not wrong to use a headlock as a form of attack, you can leave yourself in a vulnerable position if your opponent knows how to escape.

From a defensive standpoint, it is important as a grappler to know how to escape when you are caught in a headlock. Many fighters, including experienced grapplers, have sometimes been caught out in this frustrating position. BJJ does not teach any headlock techniques using the traditional methods, only variations that will not leave you compromised if your opponent escapes. BJJ only teaches how to escape headlocks, so that its practitioners can capitalize on this situation should it happen to them.

There are many headlock variations and techniques that can be taught, so here we will cover just a few of the most common situations. This will give you a good grounding in what to do and what not to do regarding headlocks. You will also grasp the fundamental details regarding the correct positioning of your body and arms, which will enable you to learn the more advanced techniques and escapes more easily at a later stage.

Submission

Headlock escape — scenario 1

As you become more advanced in jiu jitsu, you will learn that prevention is always better than cure. Not getting stuck or caught in a bad situation in the first place is always your objective. If you do find that you get caught in the worst case scenario, you will always find your correct escape route by following the escape sequences taught in this book and by your BJJ instructor.

A   In this scenario, you have been caught in a headlock by your opponent (in blue). The first thing you should do is to protect your arms by keeping them close to your body. Use your foot on the ground to move your hips away, so that you are on your side as much as possible.

B   Make a frame in front of your opponent's neck by bringing your top arm in front of his neck and holding your wrist with your other hand. Push your forearm upward into your opponent's neck to prevent him from bringing his head down.

C   Use your foot on the ground to move your hips away farther to create more space between you and your opponent. This is seen here from an aerial view for clarity.

D   You should then be able to bring your leg up and over in front of your opponent's face. Now use your leg to push your opponent away and break his grip around your neck.

E Control one of your opponent's arms and brace his body with your other hand to move your hips away. Then put one leg on either side of your opponent's neck.

F To finish the move, cross your ankles and apply pressure by stretching your legs to straighten them, choking your opponent's neck until he taps.

Submission

Headlock escape — scenario 2

Whenever you are grabbed in a headlock, you should always start out by trying to make a frame on your opponent's neck. This advice would only differ if your opponent decided to change his attack or decided not to let go of his grip around your neck. Both this and the following scenario can lead to a submission after your opponent has released his grip on your neck.

A   In this scenario you (in white) have made a frame in front of your opponent's neck, but as you attempt to push him away with your legs, he does not let go of the headlock.

B   Keep your leg in front of your opponent's face and let go of your frame. Rest your elbow on the ground and then use your leg to push your opponent's head away.

C   Still in the headlock, follow your opponent up and over, coming onto the top position.

D   Take your leg off your opponent and use your hands to make a solid base, sitting back so that you don't lose your balance and fall forward.

(Continued)

(Continued)

E   Use your hand to push down on your opponent's legs.

F   Change the position of your hips slightly and step your leg over to the mount position, keeping your hand on your opponent's leg.

G   Once mounted, put your hands on the floor to again make a solid base.

H   When your balance is stable, remake the frame on your opponent's neck.

I   To make your opponent let go of the headlock, use your forearm to drive the weight down and forward into the neck and toward the top of your opponent's head.

It is important not to let your frame collapse as you put pressure on the neck.

Submission

Headlock escape — scenario 3

The final move in this sequence differs slightly in that you cannot make your frame across the neck, because your opponent's head is next to yours. As with all techniques in BJJ, the headlock escapes will work if the situation changes and you have to adjust your techniques to compensate.

A   This time your opponent (in blue) has put his head close to yours, making it difficult for you to make your frame.

B   Hold your arm around your opponent's shoulder and hook your foot inside his leg.

C   Climb around your opponent's back and pull yourself onto the top position.

D   Now in the top position, untangle your leg and use your hands on the ground for a base. You can then move sideways into the mount position.

(Continued)

E

F

(Continued)

E–F From this reverse angle, we can see how you should check your base so that you don't fall or lose your balance. You can then make your frame on your opponent's neck.

G To make your opponent let go of the headlock, use your forearm to drive the weight down and forward into the neck and toward the top of your opponent's head. Don't let your frame collapse as you apply the pressure.

G

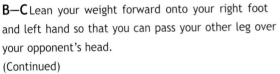

Submission

Armlock to finish

Now that your opponent has released his grip, you can capitalize by finishing with an armlock.

A   Your opponent (in blue) has let go of the headlock. Slide your head and shoulder to your opponent's wrist and bring your arm across, placing it on your shoulder. Place your other hand on the ground in front of your opponent's face.

B–C Lean your weight forward onto your right foot and left hand so that you can pass your other leg over your opponent's head.

(Continued)

(Continued)

D   To apply the lock, sit back onto the ground and then control your opponent's wrist with both hands.

E   To apply pressure on the lock, keep your knees together while raising your hips upward, while at the same time bringing your opponent's wrist downward toward your chest until he taps.

D

E

Submission

Choke from behind to finish

Another option, once your opponent has released you from the headlock, is to go for the choke if he decides to turn away from you and give you his back.

A   Anytime your opponent (in white) turns his back to you, you can take advantage by bringing one arm around his neck, making sure that your elbow is in line with his chin.

B   Hold the bicep of your other arm underneath and around your opponent's neck.

(Continued)

(Continued)

C Bring your other hand behind your opponent's neck and bring your head close to the back of your opponent's head.

D To finish the choke, bring your opponent in close to your chest while at the same time lifting him up by the neck.

If your opponent lets go during the move

Sometimes when you are in the process of escaping, your opponent may feel vulnerable and release his headlock hold. This will make your job easier, as you now no longer need to complete your escape technique because your opponent has let go of your head.

If your opponent releases when you are on the bottom you can easily move to his back, which for him can be a big disadvantage as he is vulnerable to being choked from behind. Taking somebody's back in jiu jitsu is considered to be one of the best attacking situations you can find yourself in.

If you are on the top position during your escape of the headlock and your opponent lets go, one of two things can happen. First, he can lie on his back, in which case you simply go to the mount position, and second, he can turn onto his stomach. If he lets go and turns onto his front, you simply let him turn and take his back.

Take-downs and throws

As with any BJJ technique, your base, posture and balance are the most important factors here. Unbalancing your opponent at the beginning of the fight can give you a very distinct advantage, so it's well worth mastering these techniques. Great care should be taken when practicing, as many injuries occur from falling or landing badly. Always ensure safety precautions are taken when practicing throws or take-downs.

Hip throw

The hip throw is common to many grappling arts, and it is a very effective way to develop your grips, control and balance. BJJ uses leverage from the hips and legs as opposed to speed and power, so this technique is a useful weapon.

A Start standing with your opponent (in white). You should both have a firm base and be gripping each other's elbow and collar, as shown.

B Let go of your opponent's collar and make a circular movement with your hand, starting to reach under your opponent's arm.

(Continued)

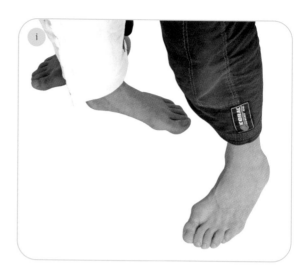

(Continued)

C   Step forward with your leading leg and move to your opponent's side by holding his belt while keeping your head close to his chest.

i   Note the position that your feet should be in — take your left leg with you so that you retain your base.

D   Step your leg in front of your opponent and reposition your hips so that you are directly in front of him.

E–F   To execute the throw, bend your knees slightly to drop your hips. You then lift your opponent up and bring your head toward your knees, taking him over while maintaining a solid base and posture.

Double leg take-down

The double leg take-down is executed from a distance when you have no grip on your partner's *gi* (uniform). It is an extremely effective way of taking your opponent to the ground.

A You and your opponent (in black) are facing each other.

B Nudge your opponent's hands up to clear your path as you make a step forward. Drop onto your knee and continue pushing your opponent's arms up.

C With your left knee between your opponent's legs, bring your other leg forward and to the outside, around to the right. Make a grip behind your opponent's knees.

D From the reverse angle, we can clearly see here how your back should be straight and your head up. (Continued)

(Continued)

E—F Keeping your back straight and your head up, stand up from a squat position.

G To finish the take-down, push your hips forward, arch your back slightly and bring your opponent's legs up under your chin.

H—I You can now finish the move, end up on top and continue your attacks.

CONCLUSION

Now that you know the theory behind Brazilian jiu jitsu, my advice as an instructor — and all good instructors will tell you the same — is that repetition is the very best way to learn. The best way for you to improve, understand and gain confidence in BJJ is to review the techniques again from the start.

Back to the beginning

Go back to the beginning and repeat each technique as if it is the first time you have seen it. More often than not, many people find that they have missed a very important detail the first, second or even the third time around. Your brain can only take in a certain amount of information at any one given time, so always allow some time between training sessions for techniques to absorb properly, and come back to them repeatedly in order to drum them into your mind. Constantly review until you no longer need to refer to the book for guidance. This should be your aim, as up until that point you may not have truly grasped the technical information sufficiently.

Take your time when practicing. Many people have a tendency to speed up when they feel they know the move, even after only seeing it once or twice. They rush to get to the next technique, thinking that the more they know, the better they will be. In BJJ, as in so many other things, quality is much better than quantity. Let speed come naturally through familiarization, repetition and relaxed practice.

Gaining a solid grasp of the basic movements and techniques in BJJ will allow you to learn the difficult moves and techniques much more easily. You will also be able to perform the advanced moves with much more finesse when your basic techniques are solid. Try to make your movements crisp as you practice, and perform them in a relaxed manner, minimizing the amount of strength or power you use. Trying to perform each technique in a relaxed way is without a doubt one of the most difficult things to accomplish in the art of BJJ.

Putting it all together

Focus on developing things such as leverage, endurance and timing. One of the beauties of Brazilian jiu jitsu is that the techniques were developed in such a way that you do not need to apply a massive amount of effort to perform them. BJJ was modified and adapted to be utilized by the smaller person, and one of Hélio Gracie's philosophies was that if it would work for someone of his size and frailty, it would work for just about anybody. Hélio's major argument was that if your opponent is bigger, heavier and stronger than you are and you try to match him for strength, speed or power, you will lose. It is for this reason that so much emphasis is placed on developing your technique, as leverage will always outmatch strength.

Your objective from the outset of your training should be to do everything to the best of your ability, never settling for anything less than 100 percent. There are no shortcuts to achieving a high standard — it will take time and dedication for you to become skilled with your techniques, but the rewards will more than compensate for your efforts. The saying "you only get out what you put in" is never a more relevant statement than when you are learning and developing your BJJ techniques.

Finally, try to have fun as you train, and learn to enjoy the sport. Many people miss out on important aspects of their development because they take learning and training far too seriously. You will absorb information more effectively and you will learn and develop just as much — if not more — when you have fun and enjoy your training sessions. There will be plenty of opportunities for you to train seriously as you progress and improve. Loving the sport is the first step to becoming proficient in it, and it is much more easy to excel when you are passionate about it.

A fighting chance of success

Around 80 percent of all fights end up on the ground in comparison to around 20 percent that are fought standing up. In this book we have deliberately covered more of the ground situations that you might find yourself in, rather than the standing scenarios.

The ground is the most neglected and most misunderstood area of a fight. Some people are overreliant on kicks and punches and think that they will not end up on the ground, but it is actually far more likely that a fight will consist of two people rolling around on the floor grappling rather than exchanging kicks and punches from a standing position. Most fights start from a standing position, and while knowing how to strike effectively is important, knowing how to grapple and take your opponent down and being able to defend his throws and take-down attempts is equally as important.

The reality of most street fights is that the two combatants end up grabbing onto each other, scrambling around and then simply tripping and falling over. In a real fight it is likely that we have no control over how it will start and what will happen — all we can do is prepare ourselves for all eventualities. BJJ is very well known for its ground capabilities but it also has many standing techniques, which include throws and take-downs, that you can include in your arsenal as you become a more accomplished grappler. More importantly, though, it is better to start from the ground techniques and work your way up from the floor to the standing positions.

Take-downs and throws really become relevant in a sporting context when two skilled competitors are trying to establish dominance and control over each other in a controlled environment. They are trying to win in a specific way because of the rules of the competition, which will determine a winner by a throw or take-down, a pinning of the opponent on their back or outscoring the opponent on a points system. Some martial arts, such as judo, sambo and wrestling, concentrate 80 percent of their training time working on throws, take-downs and pins, although this percentage will vary slightly from school to school. When they have completed their objective they stop and start from the standing position all over again.

In Brazilian jiu jitsu the fight is allowed to continue after the throw or the take-down until there is a winner by submission or by points at the end of the allotted time. BJJ fighters are also encouraged to improve their position or submit their opponent, and this is probably one of the reasons for much of its success in cage fighting and mixed martial arts competitions.

Final word — how I started

I have been practicing and teaching martial arts for approximately 18 years. I started out in karate and kickboxing and practiced religiously and happily for many years. It was in 1995 that my life in martial arts made a major turnaround after watching the Ultimate Fighting Championship. Like many others, I witnessed Royce Gracie defeating various opponents from all types of martial arts disciplines with relative ease. From that moment on, I knew that the art of Brazilian jiu jitsu was for me.

My journey in BJJ has taken me all over the world in my attempts to advance and improve my technique and knowledge in grappling. I have had the great fortune of meeting, training with and learning from some of the most renowned names in BJJ. My early years of training were at the Gracie Academy in Torrance, California. The experience I gained there in those early years under Royce, Rorion and Hélio Gracie, and the many other instructors at the academy, has turned out to be priceless with regard to my long-term training goals.

I was privileged to be part of a program of development at the academy that allowed me to work alongside many great students and instructors. The help, encouragement and friendship I received from my teammates have had a major positive influence on my ability as a jiu jitsu instructor and fighter. After my formal training at the academy, I returned home to London and opened a BJJ academy in Essex. My dream was to assist and spread the art of Brazilian jiu jitsu in Great Britain. I began to build a student base and have slowly seen BJJ grow from almost nothing into one of the most popular martial arts in the United Kingdom today.

As my academy expanded, I was fortunate enough to meet one of the most humble, quietly unassuming and knowledgeable BJJ instructors of our time. Mauricio Motta Gomes was a representative of Gracie-Barra in England and, like myself, was also trying to establish BJJ in the United Kingdom. Mauricio was one of only a handful of people to be given his black belt by the late, legendary Rolls Gracie, one of the innovators of BJJ before his unfortunate and untimely death in a hang-gliding accident.

Mauricio soon became my teacher, mentor and friend. His unselfishness in passing on his knowledge, coupled with his experience and teaching ability, has helped me to excel at a level that I could only dream of. Despite the great amount of knowledge I have accumulated to date, I still always learn from Mauricio. This is because of his attention to detail in the execution of BJJ techniques and the fact that he wants only the best from his students.

Training with Mauricio and the Gracie-Barra team has opened many doors for me and enabled me to train with and learn from some of the best fighters in the BJJ world — among them many renowned teachers and world BJJ champions, such as Roger Gracie (Mauricio's son), Carlos Gracie Jr (the pioneer of Gracie-Barra), Marcio Feitosa, Carlos Lemos, Gordo, Braulio Estima, Felip Souza, Joao Angel and Ze Radiola, to mention just a few.

What I have learned above all, and hope to pass on to you, is that the learning curve in jiu jitsu is neverending. I have discovered that every situation has something to teach me. We learn not just from the oldest, most experienced fighters, but from the newest and least experienced as well.

Jiu jitsu has taught me many things about myself that have nothing to do with fighting — I have gained confidence, honesty, loyalty, discipline, patience and commitment. My hope within the pages of this book is to convey to you not just the rewards of mastering a sweep, an armlock or a choke, but what jiu jitsu teaches us about ourselves, which has the ability to develop and enrich our minds. The philosophy of jiu jitsu has taught me to deal not just with combat situations but with life experiences as well. Jiu jitsu helps you to look at difficult situations in your life from different perspectives and try to find simple solutions to them, rather than being heavy-handed or aggressive. BJJ is a way of life, not just a martial art, and I hope you come to love it as much as I do.

Marc Walder

A BLACK BELT IS JUST A BEGINNER WHO DIDN'T QUIT!

GLOSSARY

BASE	Position in which your posture is correct and your balance firm
BJJ	Brazilian jiu jitsu. A form of martial art adapted in Brazil by the Gracie family from the traditional Japanese art of jiu jitsu. It promotes the principle that a smaller, weaker person can successfully defend themselves against a larger, stronger opponent
CAGE FIGHTING	UFC event conducted in an octagonal caged arena where professional fighters test their skills against one another in a no-holds-barred match
CARLOS GRACIE	Taught jiu jitsu by Mitsuyo Maeda and went on to teach his brother, Hélio
CHOKE HOLD	Or stranglehold. A grappling hold that strangles the opponent and leads to loss of consciousness. Should be applied with care
DRILL	A form of exercise practicing a jiu jitsu movement used in warm-up exercises
GI	Traditional cotton kimono-style uniform worn by martial artists when practicing techniques and training
GRACIE BARRA	Academy in Rio de Janeiro formed by Carlos Gracie Jr
GRACIE FAMILY	Founders of BJJ

GRACIE JIU JITSU	*See* Brazilian jiu jitsu. Specifically refers to the style taught by Rorion Gracie and his selected teachers
GRAPPLE	To wrestle with and control an opponent on the ground, without the use of striking
HÉLIO GRACIE	Taught jiu jitsu by his brother Carlos, and developed BJJ along with him as a means of using his slight, frail physique to the best advantage
JIU JITSU	An art of either attacking or defending using one's own body
JOINT LOCK	A grappling technique that involves isolating an opponent's limb and creating a lever with your own body position that will force the joint past its normal range of motion. Can cause injury if applied suddenly or forcefully
JUDO	A derivative of jiu jitsu
KODOKAN	The headquarters of the judo world, literally meaning "a place for the study or promotion of the way." Established by the founder of judo, Jigoro Kano, in 1882. Now located in Tokyo, Japan

GLOSSARY

MITSUYO MAEDA	Also known as "Count Combat" or *Conde Koma*. A Japanese member of the Kodokan and expert judoka who emigrated to Brazil in the 1910s and met Gastão Gracie, teaching his son Carlos jiu jitsu	**SUBMISSION**	To formally give up by tapping out verbally or physically when your opponent has caught you in a joint lock or choke hold
MMA	Mixed martial arts. A combination of martial arts styles used together in a combat situation	**SUBMISSION HOLD**	A technique or move that brings about a submission, usually a joint lock or choke
ROYCE GRACIE	Professional MMA fighter and BJJ practitioner. Became well-known in the mid-1990s for his huge success at the UFC over larger, stronger fighters of all disciplines. Popularized BJJ and and ground fighting techniques around the world	**TAKE-DOWN/THROW**	To take your opponent to the ground from a standing position
		TAP/TAP OUT	To let your partner know that you wish to give up by physically banging your hand or foot on the opponent or on the ground. You may also give up verbally by telling your opponent that you wish to stop
SCISSOR	To use your limbs in a scissor-like motion to perform a movement	**TRAP**	To block, control or hold a limb
		UFC	Ultimate Fighting Championship. The original MMA event where no-rules fighting originated
SPARRING	A form of training consisting of free-form fighting, although certain rules or customs ensure that injuries are unlikely. Gives students an opportunity to test their skills and develop them under realistic conditions	**VALE TUDO**	Literally "anything goes" — describes MMA competitions in unarmed combat with minimal rules

PHOTOGRAPHIC CREDITS

All photography by Mike Holdsworth, with the exception of those supplied by the following photographers and/or agencies (copyright rests with these individuals and/or their agencies):
Page 10: Image in the public domain
Page 11: Courtesy of Wikipedia under the GNU Free Documentation License

MAKING CONTACT

INTERNATIONAL BJJ FEDERATIONS & TRAINING ASSOCIATIONS

- INTERNATIONAL BRAZILIAN JIU JITSU FEDERATION
Av Commandante Julio de Moura 267, Barra da Tijuca, Rio de Janeiro — RJ — Brazil, CEP: 22620-010
  - Tel: 55 (0XX21) 2493-4929
  - E-mail: ibjjf@ibjjf.org
  - Website: www.ibjjf.org

- EUROPEAN FIGHT NETWORK
PO Box 38189, London, W10 5WB, UK
  - Tel: 44 07092 279 089
  - E-mail: info@bjj.eu.com
  - Website: www.bjj.eu.com

AUSTRALIA
- AUSTRALIAN FEDERATION OF BRAZILIAN JIU JITSU
PO Box 280, Torquay, Victoria 3228, Australia
  - Tel: 061 3 5261 4476
  - Email: info@afbjj.com
  - Website: www.bjj.com.au

BRAZIL
- GRACIE-BARRA
Avenida Olegário Maciel 366 sala 206 Barra da Tijuca, Rio de Janeiro — RJ — CEP: 22621-200
  - Tel: 55 0XX21 3153 3694
  - Email: infogb@graciebarra.com
  - Website: www.graciebarra.com

CHINA
- BEIJING BLACK TIGER ACADEMY / GRACIE CHINA
Suite 906, Building 9, Jianwai Soho, Chaoyang District, Beijing, PRC 100022
  - Tel: 86 1368 140 2122
  - Email: admin@blacktigerclub.com
  - Website: www.graciechina.com

CANADA
- ALLIANCE BRAZILIAN JIU JITSU
113 Charles Street West, 3rd Floor, Kitchener, Ontario, Canada
  - Tel: 001 519 505 3692
  - Email: eric@alliancebjj.ca
  - Website: www.alliancebjj.ca

UK
- GRACIE BARRA UK FIGHT TEAM
PO Box 38189, London, W10 5WB, UK
  - Tel: 44 07092 279 089
  - Email: london@gracie-barra.co.uk
  - Website: www.gracie-barra.co.uk

- BRÁULIO ESTIMA
14 Neston Grive, Stechford, Birmingham, UK
  - Tel: 044 77 8696 4932
  - Website: www.braulioestima.net

- BRAZILIAN JIU JITSU UK
Sleeping Storm Dojo, Hook Road, Epsom, Surrey, KT19 8TU, UK
  - Tel: 044 1372 749 458
  - E-mail: info@brazilianjiu-jitsu.co.uk
  - Website: www.brazilianjiu-jitsu.co.uk

USA
- UNITED STATES JIU JITSU FEDERATION
23 Spectrum Pointe Drive, Suite 205, Lake Forest, CA 92630
  - Tel: 949 678 1259
  - E-mail: usjjf@usjjf.com
  - Website: www.usjjf.com

- GRACIE BARRA
23 Spectrum Pointe Drive, Suite 205, Lake Forest, CA 92630
  - Tel: 949 795 5257
  - E-mail: infogb@graciebarra.com
  - Website: www.graciebarraamerica.com

INTERNATIONAL BJJ FEDERATIONS & TRAINING ASSOCIATIONS

- RICKSON GRACIE
15332 Antioch Street, Ste #831,
Pacific Palisades, CA 90272
- Tel: 310 914 4122
- E-mail:
rgjjcenter@rickson.com
- Website: www.rickson.com

- ROYCE GRACIE
PO Box 10346, Torrance, CA
90505
- Tel: 310 316 4579
- E-mail:
roycegracie@roycegracie.tv
- Website:
www.roycegracie.tv

- RODRIGO GRACIE
c/o Mike Kogan, East Coast
Office, 9806 Zackary Avenue,
Charlotte, NC 28277
- Tel: 704 996 9301
- E-mail: mk@roycegracie.tv
- Website:
www.rodrigogracie.com

- RENZO GRACIE JIU JITSU
224 West 30th Street, New
York, NY
- Tel: 212 279 6724
- E-mail:
info@renzogracie.com
- Website:
www.renzogracie.com

- GRACIE JIU JITSU ACADEMY
3515 Artesia Boulevard,
Torrance, CA 90504
- Tel: 310 353 4100
- E-mail:
info@gracieacademy.com
- Website:
www.gracieacademy.com

- RICARDO ALMEIDA BRAZILIAN
JIU JITSU ACADEMY
2619 Broad Street, Hamilton,
NJ 08610
- Tel: 609 888 2121
- E-mail:
info@ricardoalmeida.com
- Website:
www.ricardoalmeida.com

- CAIQUE JIU JITSU ACADEMY
19751 South Figueroa Street,
Carson, CA 90745
- Tel: 310 618 8149
- E-mail:
besafe@caiquejiujitsu.com
- Website:
www.caiquejiujitsu.com

- SERRA BRAZILIAN JIU JITSU
2554 Hempstead Turnpike, East
Meadow, NY 11554
- Tel: 516 520 2052
- Website:
www.serrajitsu.com

- BOSTON BRAZILIAN JIU JITSU
10 Dedham Street, Newton,
MA 02461
- Tel: 617 969 9901
- Website:
www.bbjiujitsu.com

MAKING CONTACT

USEFUL WEBSITES

Fight news from around the world.
- www.adcombat.com

Kevlar clothing approved and endorsed by Royce Gracie and used around the world by various police forces and security agencies.
- www.bladerunner.tv

Grapplers Quest — news about the grappling show and its latest events.
- www.grapplers.com

Marc Walder Jiu Jitsu — news, useful links and training times for his classes in Brazilian jiu jitsu.
- www.bjj-online.com

Mixed martial arts website featuring news, interviews, pictures, statistics and everything else you need to know about MMA.
- www.sherdog.com

Clothing suitable for all BJJ and martial arts enthusiasts.
- www.44adclothing.com

USEFUL WEBSITES

Test your knowledge of mixed martial arts.

- www.mmatrivia.com

Find out everything you ever wanted to know about the Ultimate Fighting Championships.

- www.ufc.com

Clothing for female fighters, made by female fighters.

- www.alphafemalefight wear.com

Details and links for Brazilian jiu jitsu clubs and academies throughout Europe.

- http://sfuk.tripod.com/ bjjclubs.html

Brazilian jiu jitsu news, reviews, techniques and more.

- www.bjjfighter.com

Brazilian jiu jitsu news and merchandise.

- www.onthemat.com

Gis and other clothing.

- www.mmauniverse.com